"The choice, not the motive. This is the pivotal point of Emil Sher's wrenching drama.... This is not a play that sets out to answer the unanswerable question of what any one of us might do in the same situation. But it is a play that warrants many more productions and subsequent discussions."
—Iris Winston, *Variety*

"The hippo scene is the first moment in Emil Sher's drama *Mourning Dove* when the audience is put on notice that all lazy and off-the-shelf moral judgments about Robert Latimer and why he killed his severely disabled daughter must be set aside.... Sher's script, Lorne Pardy's directing and the... actors... offer no guidance whatsoever toward reaching moral consensus on Latimer's act. Why? Because there is none. They merely illustrate how complex the responses of the human heart and human soul are."
—Michael Valpy, *The Globe and Mail*

"It's extremely well written. That's what really hit me first of all. Emil Sher has avoided all the traps of high melodrama and false sentimentality.... He shows, in fact, all possible attitudes and he avoids preaching very, very well.... ... [He] does not allow us to get too caught up in the tragedy of the event... by introducing the third character, Keith.... He makes non-stop jokes, so the despair that hangs over the family is constantly disrupted by this very disturbing humour produced by Keith. And the humour creates a distance that forces us to think about the situation as much as to feel it."
—Alvina Ruprecht, *Ottawa Morning*, CBC Radio

"Sher holds back from moral judgment in this play, but I certainly felt one in the gunshot-loud slamming of a door as Sandra enters to confront her husband. There is no equivocation in this moment. The ambiguity begins after this apparent point of no return. Doug... has done what she herself once contemplated. In that choice they are divided. But why *did* she choose differently, Sandra wonders. Out of cowardice? Out of love? Which one of them was Tina's true protector?"
—Ann Marie Todkill, *Canadian Medical Association Journal*

MOURNING DOVE

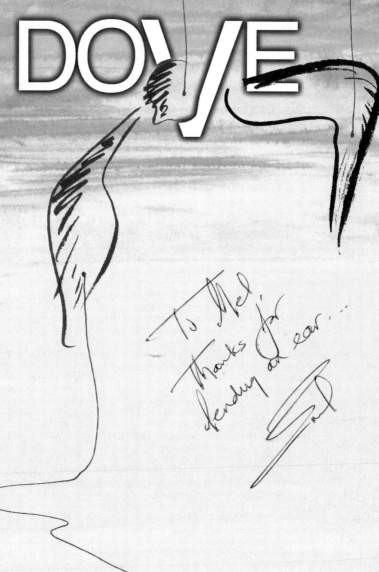

To Mel,
Thanks for
lending an ear...

Mourning Dove

Emil Sher

Playwrights Canada Press
Toronto • Canada

Playwrights Canada Press
215 Spadina Ave. Toronto, Ontario CANADA M5T 2C7
416.703.0013 fax 416.408.3402
orders@playwrightscanada.com • www.playwrightscanada.com

Playwrights Canada Press acknowledges the financial support of the Canadian
taxpayer through the Government of Canada Book Publishing Industry
Development Programme (BPIDP) for our publishing activities.
We also acknowledge the Canadian and Ontario taxpayers through the
Canada Council for the Arts and the Ontario Arts Council.

Cover art by David Rayfield
Production Editor: MZK

Library and Archives Canada Cataloguing in Publication

Sher, Emil, 1959-
        Mourning dove / Emil Sher.

A play.
ISBN 0-88754-766-4

     1. Euthanasia--Drama. 2. People with disabilities--Drama. I. Title.

PS8587.H38535M69 2005   C812'.54   C2005-902920-X

First edition: May 2005.
Printed and bound by Printco at Scarborough, Canada.

For Kathryn

Production notes

Mourning Dove, based on an original radio play of the same name, is inspired by a true story, but the dramatic world in which the story is set is entirely fictional. In the radio drama the role of Keith was played by an actor with Down's syndrome. The stage version does not need to meet the same criteria. What is essential, however, is that Keith be portrayed as someone who is mildly developmentally handicapped, and has been marginalised because of his condition.

Tina is portrayed by an off-stage actor and, consequently, she is never seen. Yet all the characters interact with Tina as if she was sitting in her wheelchair. Her presence is felt throughout the play by a pool of light and by virtue of her breathing. The light and her breathing surface as she enters a scene and fade as she exits. Her dialogue is not a matter of text as it is texture: the range and rhythms of her every breath.

Mourning Dove premiered at the Great Canadian Theatre Company in Ottawa on February 17, 2005 with the following cast and creative team:

Doug Ramsay	Timothy Webber
Sandra Ramsay	Kate Hurman
Tina Ramsay	Stephanie Burchell
Keith Martel	Ben Meuser
Director	Lorne Pardy
Set & Costume Designer	Kim Nielsen
Lighting Designer	Leigh Ann Vardy
Composer	Duncan Morgan
Stage Manager	Shainna Laviolette
Assistant Director	Sandra McNeill
Fight Choreographer	John Koensgen
Lighting Operator	Shane Learmouth
Sound Operator	Jon Carter
Wardrobe & Props	Sarah Feely
Production Manager	Rachel Fancy
Apprentice Stage Manager	Kevin Waghorn
Head Scenic Painter	Stephanie Dahmer

Characters

Doug Ramsay, 40s
Sandra Ramsay, 40s,
Tina Ramsay, 12 (voice only)
Keith Martel, late 20s: a family friend and Doug's employee

Setting

A barn-like workshop/garage behind the Ramsays' house.

The stage is black.

TINA   *Steady and anchored.*

           *TINA's slow, rhythmic breathing is suddenly
           pierced by the sound of a shrill electric saw. The
           spinning blade is relentless, unforgiving. As the
           lights come up the sound of the saw fades, melding
           with the sound of DOUG Ramsay cutting a thin
           piece of wood with a hand saw. The barn-like
           structure that serves as a work shed and garage also
           doubles as a theatre for TINA. Colourful wooden
           animal marionettes dangle from the rafters,
           reminiscent of a mobile suspended over an infant's
           crib. A large, colourful ark-shaped puppet stage is
           near completion. DOUG saws with great intensity,
           slowly drawing the saw back and forth in stops and
           starts.*

           Laborious and painful.

           *DOUG looks at TINA in response to her changed
           breathing.*

DOUG   Hey, pumpkin. What d'you think? It's just about
           finished. A few touch-ups and this ark will be ready
           to sail. We're talking a first-class show for a first-class
           daughter. The puppets, they can't wait. The bears are
           dancing. The monkeys are doing cartwheels.

TINA   *Eases back into a steady rhythm.*

           *Only when DOUG is sure TINA is fine does he
           continue sawing. The cut piece falls to the floor.*

DOUG   I'll be Noah again. Keith, he's my son, Ham.

           *DOUG picks up the cut piece. He examines it and
           holds it in his hand as if weighing it.*

You get to watch. You'll watch me round up all the animals, two by two. Well, not all the animals. It's a small ark. Not everyone can get on.

> *DOUG begins to cut the same length of wood with a singular intensity. He doesn't notice when SANDRA enters.*

SANDRA   Time for bed.

> *SANDRA walks up to DOUG.*

Bed time.

DOUG   I'm not finished.

SANDRA   Not you. Tina.

DOUG   She's not tired.

> *SANDRA walks toward TINA.*

SANDRA   She's sleeping.

DOUG   She must have just fallen asleep.

SANDRA   Good timing on her part.

DOUG   Don't…. (*beat*) Don't take her in yet.

SANDRA   Why not?

DOUG   I want her company.

SANDRA   Even if she's asleep?

DOUG   She's beautiful when she sleeps.

SANDRA   She's beautiful when she's awake.

DOUG   That's not what I meant.

SANDRA   I know exactly what you meant. Bring her in when
            you're done.

            *SANDRA walks toward the shed door, then turns
            back and points to the ark.*

            What colour is that blue?

DOUG   (*beat*) Sky blue, I guess.

SANDRA   I'm thinking of painting Tina's room. Blue trim
            around her window to go with the red birdhouse.
            'Course, the birdhouse needs a fresh coat but I'll leave
            that to Keith. (*beat*) I may not paint at all. I saw some
            really funky wallpaper the other day and boom, I'm
            this six-year old playing dollhouse, thinking of
            a million possibilities.

DOUG   When exactly did you plan on playing dollhouse?

SANDRA   When Tina's in rehab. (*beat*) After the operation.

DOUG   "Salvage procedure." That's what Dr. Kovacs called
            it. A salvage procedure.

SANDRA   I heard her.

DOUG   Sawing off Tina's thighbone like she was kindling.

SANDRA   Sshhhh!

DOUG   She's sleeping.

SANDRA   And when all this is over I don't want her sleeping in
            the same old room. Twelve-year olds like a little
            splash in their lives.

DOUG   She's got a beautiful room.

SANDRA   It's not going to be less beautiful. Just different.

DOUG busies himself with the ark.

DOUG   I don't want you renovating and rearranging.

SANDRA   I'm not gutting the house, Doug. I'm just thinkin' of sprucing up Tina's room. She deserves a little something when she gets back. Maybe a sky blue ceiling with big, fluffy clouds. Or… or a grinning moon with a thousand winking stars. (*beat*) Or one wall filled with flowers. Sunflowers with attitude. (*beat*) Sunflowers with sunglasses. (*beat*) Help me out here.

DOUG   I've got an ark to finish.

SANDRA   You've been going gangbusters. I still think the cardboard ark would've been fine.

DOUG   Not this time around.

SANDRA   All these late nights. I half-expect to find your bed in here one day. (*grins*) If I didn't know better I'd think you were having an affair.

DOUG   No lipstick on my collar. Just paint.

SANDRA   You should spend more time in the house. The three of us. (*beat*) Dr. Kovacs is going to call any day now.

DOUG   That's why I want Tina nearby.

SANDRA   So do I. (*beat*) You want me to give you a hand? Maybe speed things up.

DOUG   I'm fine. (*pause*) She's going to be okay.

SANDRA   (*beat*) Okay. (*pause*) I'm going to wait up for you.

DOUG   Have a nice, hot bath, then.

> *DOUG picks up a brush and daubs SANDRA's
> cheek with a dab of blue paint.*

You're turning blue.

> *SANDRA smiles as she wipes off the paint.*

SANDRA   Blue walls. (*beat*) Blue walls with a thousand goldfish.
(*beat*) Goldfish with red lips.

> *SANDRA exits. DOUG turns to TINA and
> savours the sight of her sleeping peacefully. He
> returns to the ark and works with a single-minded
> intensity, removed from his surroundings.*
>
> *A change in lighting reflects DOUG's move into his
> own private world, and a shift in time. He doesn't
> notice KEITH walk in. KEITH sees DOUG is
> utterly preoccupied.*

KEITH   Good morning.

> *KEITH walks to TINA. Her breathing shifts as
> KEITH sits in front of her. He begins to sand a new
> marionette he has almost completed: a large-winged
> dove.*

TINA   *Even-keeled.*

KEITH   (*to TINA*) I'm making you a mourning dove. (*louder*)
A mourning dove.

> *DOUG turns to KEITH, who looks triumphant
> now that he's punctured DOUG's thoughts.*

For when you wake up in the morning.

DOUG   It's not that kind of morning. The 'mourning' in mourning dove is spelled with a "u". As in mourning and funerals and black veils. We're talking 'mourning' with a 'u'.

KEITH   So there's no mourning-without-a-u dove?

DOUG   No.

KEITH   What about an evening dove?

DOUG   No such thing.

KEITH   How do you know? (*beat*) Maybe you saw an evening dove and thought it was a mourning dove but it was really an evening dove. Maybe you have to look real close to see what's different. Like when they show you two pictures that look the same. The first time you look at it, you think everything's the same in both pictures. A flower pot, a flower pot. A rake, a rake. You have to look a few times, then you see the flower in the second picture is missing a petal. You put a circle around what's different. Same thing with the mourning dove and the evening dove. Maybe they look the same, until you get real close.

DOUG   You'll never see an evening dove, Keith.

KEITH   If you saw a mourning-with-a-u dove at night, you could call it an evening mourning dove. Couldn't you?

DOUG   I suppose.

KEITH   (*pause*) If you saw a mourning dove in the afternoon, you could call it—

DOUG   I get the picture.

KEITH   Tina's going to see it morning, noon and night. At the rehab centre. (*to TINA*) That would be morning-with-out-a-u.

DOUG   (*pause*) You're going to want to keep it here, with all the other animals.

KEITH   No. The rehab centre. When she recovers from the operation. She'll need company. She'll need the dove and the bear and... and the Three Little Pigs.

DOUG   There's not enough room.

KEITH   They can take turns. First, the dove and the bear. Then the dove and the Three Little Pigs. Then the dove and the monkey. (*to TINA*) I hope you like it.

DOUG   She's crazy about your puppets.

KEITH   Not the puppets. Her room at the rehab centre. You think she'll like it?

DOUG   It's not a question of 'like' or 'dislike'.

KEITH   What kind of question is it, then?

DOUG   It's.... It's hard to explain.

KEITH   (*to TINA*) It's far.

DOUG   Too far.

KEITH   (*to TINA*) I won't be able to see you. Not every day.

DOUG   No.

KEITH   (*to TINA*) That's why you'll need the dove. The dove will always be there. Because we can't.

DOUG   What you have to set your mind on is the show.

KEITH	Are you finished yet? The script.
DOUG	Almost.
KEITH	I have a big part.
DOUG	As always.
KEITH	(*pause*) Can I be Noah this time?
DOUG	I'm Noah.
KEITH	I know-a. Get it? I know-a good place to go fishing.
DOUG	I get it.
KEITH	That would be 'know' with a 'k'. (*beat*) Why do we have silent letters? (*to TINA*) Like the 'k' in 'knob'. Or knife. Or…
DOUG	Knowledge.
KEITH	Knowledge. Why do we need 'em if we don't use 'em? Silent letters.
DOUG	I didn't invent language, Keith.
KEITH	Who did?
DOUG	You keep yammering away and I'll never get this done. Is that what you want?
KEITH	I want you to finish.
DOUG	I want to finish.
KEITH	I'm glad I'm not you.
DOUG	What's that supposed to mean?

KEITH   I'm glad I never play Noah. I like it when I'm Little Red Riding Hood. Or the Giant. (*to TINA*) "Fee, Fi, Fo, Fum, I smell the blood of an Englishman." (*to DOUG*) Noah always has to decide. Two zebras. Two elephants. Two dogs. What do you tell all the other zebras and elephants and dogs?

DOUG   You tell them not all choices are easy to make.

KEITH   Choosing isn't fair. (*pause*) Noah could choose not to choose. He could say, "No." (*beat*) He says, "No!" a lot. (*beat*) Maybe that's why he's called No-ah.

DOUG   Maybe.

KEITH   (*pause*) A hundred hippos means ninety-eight No's.

> *KEITH stands and walks laterally as if talking to a line of hippos, taking a step between each "No."*

No. No. No. No. No. No. No. No.

DOUG   There's only so much room on the ark.

KEITH   Build a bigger ark.

DOUG   It doesn't work that way.

KEITH   Make it work.

DOUG   You make it sound so easy.

KEITH   You make it sound so hard. (*pause*) I couldn't do it. I couldn't do it. I couldn't decide.

DOUG   You don't have to, Keith.

KEITH   We don't have two of everything.

DOUG   We don't need two of everything. It's a short play.

KEITH   One dove is enough?

DOUG   One dove is fine.

KEITH   (*to TINA*) I'm waiting for the eyes. (*beat*) You can buy
         eyes, you know. I was going to use buttons but then
         Sandra told me about the eyes. Plastic eyes you can
         buy. She told me to try Crenshaw's, and I did and
         they had eyes but they didn't have the eyes I wanted.
         They said they'd order more.

DOUG   You can always paint the eyes.

KEITH   I want the dove to be special. (*to TINA*) 'Cause it's a
         special event.

DOUG   The show of all shows.

KEITH   Not the show. The operation.

DOUG   You're thinking the operation is a 'special event'.

KEITH   What'd'you call it, then?

DOUG   (*beat*) Unfair.

                SANDRA enters through the shed door.

SANDRA   Is that old fishbowl in here?

KEITH   (*grins*) For some old fish?

SANDRA   For Tina. (*to TINA*) We're going to fill it up with all
         your special things.

DOUG   Why?

SANDRA   For her room at the rehab. We'll put all of Tina's
         favourite bits and pieces in it and take it with.

KEITH   Like peaches. Peaches in a jar. You put them in jars so you can eat them in winter.

           KEITH hunts around the shed for a large jar.

DOUG   I haven't seen that fishbowl in ages.

KEITH   (holding a large, lidded jar) How's this?

DOUG   (*beat*) I need that.

SANDRA   (laughs) For what?

KEITH   I need it.

DOUG   If I didn't need it I'd have thrown it out long ago. It's here, so it's needed.

SANDRA   (still laughing) That's not logic. That's an excuse for this clutter.

           SANDRA looks for the fishbowl. KEITH returns to his spot in front of TINA. He holds the dove in one hand and the jar in the other as he launches into an impromptu puppet show.

KEITH   (*to TINA*) One day, a dove found a message in a bottle. "Oh, boy," said the dove. "A bottle with a message in it! I wonder what it says."

SANDRA   What should we put inside Tina's jar of goodies?

           KEITH's monologue runs beneath DOUG and SANDRA's conversation.

KEITH   The dove wanted to read the message inside the bottle. But she couldn't get the cork out. "What am I going to do?" said the dove. "I want to read the message in the bottle but the cork is stuck. Stuck, stuck, stuck." So the dove… the dove…. The dove decided to break the bottle. 'Cause it's what's inside that counts.

DOUG   (*beat*) What she needs can't fit inside a jar.

SANDRA   I'll start. (*pause*) Her chimes. Your turn.

DOUG   (*pause*) Her blinking stars.

SANDRA   (*beat*) Her wind-up penguin.

DOUG   Her jack-in-the-box.

SANDRA   It doesn't work anymore.

DOUG   I used it the other night.

SANDRA   It doesn't work on Tina. Not with me it didn't. (*beat*) My turn.

KEITH   So she took the bottle in her beak and... and smashed it against a rock. Bang! Bang! Bang!

TINA   *Suddenly clipped, suggesting she's startled.*

>   *DOUG, SANDRA and KEITH all respond by ensuring TINA is all right.*

Eases into a constant rhythm.

>   *The conversation and play resume.*

KEITH   And the bottle broke. And inside was a message.

DOUG   I say we do this some other time.

SANDRA   I say we get a bigger jar.

KEITH   The dove took the message and, and unfolded it.

SANDRA   I'd take her whole room if I could.

KEITH   And the message said. *(beat)* The message said…

DOUG   Decide what matters most.

KEITH   *(beat)* "Decide what matters most." *(beat)* The end! *(holds jar up to DOUG)* Can I keep this?

DOUG   What for?

KEITH   I need it. For the play.

SANDRA   You take it, Keith.

KEITH   What about the fishbowl?

SANDRA   I thought of something else.

> *KEITH takes the jar and exits through the shed door.*

Her "T" box. *(beat)* It's perfect.

> *SANDRA exits. DOUG watches TINA and listens to her subdued breathing. TINA's breathing slowly fades.*

> *Lights shift. DOUG puts on a cloak that suggests he's Noah. KEITH enters, wearing the headdress from his biblical costume. He walks to the ramp and waits for his cue.*

DOUG   Ham, position the ramp.

> *KEITH doesn't move.*

Ham, position the ramp.

> *KEITH continues to stand still.*

(*low*) You're Ham.

KEITH   I'm not Ham any more.

DOUG   'Course you are.

KEITH   I changed my mind.

DOUG   You didn't tell me.

KEITH   You didn't ask.

DOUG   I don't have to ask. I'm Noah. You're Ham. You've always been Ham. That's how it's written.

KEITH   You can unwrite it. (*beat*) I want to be the other son this time.

DOUG   Shem or Japheth?

KEITH   Shem. I like Shem. (*beat*) Ham makes me feel like a sandwich.

DOUG   All right. We'll make it Shem. (*beat*) You make any other changes I should know about?

KEITH shakes his head.

Shem, position the ramp.

KEITH   Yes, father.

KEITH maneuvers the ramp.

How's this?

DOUG   Perfect. (*beat*) Tell me, Shem. Have you spoken with Hippo?

KEITH   Yes, father.

DOUG   And?... (*beat*) And?...

KEITH   And I forgot my line.

DOUG   "Hippo dug his heels in."

KEITH   Hippo dug his heels in.

DOUG   You must speak to him.

KEITH   (*beat*) Do hippos have heels?

DOUG   What?

KEITH   Do hippos have heels?

DOUG   It's an expression, Keith. (*beat*) Bring Hippo to me.

KEITH   Yes, father.

> *KEITH walks to the side of the shed and picks up a small, stuffed hippo. He carries the hippo over to the foot of the ramp.*

Hippo is here, father.

DOUG   Thank you, Shem. (*beat*) Hippo, Shem tells me you don't want to join us on the ark. Is this true?

KEITH   Yes.

DOUG   You don't want to leave your brothers behind.

KEITH   No.

DOUG   I understand. Come up the ramp. We'll talk.

> *KEITH doesn't move the hippo.*

Come up, Hippo. We'll talk.

> *KEITH keeps the hippo still.*

> This is important, Keith. Up the ramp, then down. Up, then back down. Up, down. Up, down. Up, down. That's what Tina needs. The motion, it makes her laugh. You know what she's like when you make that hippo dance. (*beat*) Come up, Hippo. We'll talk.

KEITH   You never used to talk to Hippo. (*beat*) Noah doesn't speak hippo.

DOUG   He doesn't have to.

KEITH   Maybe Hippo doesn't want to go on the ark because no one knows how to speak hippo.

DOUG   There's gonna be one other hippo.

KEITH   You still won't know what they're thinking.

DOUG   Look. God tells Noah, 'Round up all the animals two by two'. He doesn't say 'Make sure you learn how to speak hippo.' (*beat*) We're doing this for Tina.

KEITH   To make Tina laugh.

DOUG   You betcha.

KEITH   The hippo makes her laugh.

DOUG   The hippo going up and down the ramp. That always does the trick. (*beat*) You ready to try again?

KEITH   Ready.

DOUG   Come up, Hippo. We'll talk.

> *KEITH inches the hippo up at a glacial pace.*

> A little faster, Keith.

KEITH   Shem.

DOUG   A little faster, Shem. (*beat*) Faster than that.

　　　　　　KEITH lifts the hippo and moves it to and fro as if it's flying.

　　　　　　You don't want it to fly, now.

KEITH   Why not?

DOUG   Hippos don't have wings.

KEITH   Hippos don't have heels.

DOUG   Maybe so, but… but your dove, for instance. You're going to want your dove to fly.

KEITH   My dove doesn't have eyes.

DOUG   Not yet. But when it does, you're going to want it to fly. You watch Tina's face when you move those wings.

KEITH   She'll love the flying Hippo, too.

DOUG   I don't want Hippo flying.

KEITH   Why not?

DOUG   If Hippo is flying it means he's not listening. Hippo has to listen to what Noah is saying. He has to hear Noah's explanation. (*beat*) It's all in the script.

KEITH   We can change the script.

DOUG   We keep changing things and we'll never be ready.

KEITH   We never had one before. A script.

DOUG   We never needed one.

KEITH   I don't like scripts.

DOUG   This isn't about you, Keith.

> *KEITH grabs hold of a vibrant, papier-mâché stalk, tall as a ladder.*

KEITH   I want to do Jack and the Beanstalk. (*beat*) Fee, Fi, Fo, Fum. I smell the blood of—

DOUG   (*firm*) Not this time.

KEITH   She loves the Three Little Pigs. (*beat*) "I'll huff, and I'll puff, and I'll blooooooooow your house—"

DOUG   (*cuts him off*) We're doing the Noah story.

KEITH   (*beat*) Can I huff and puff in the Noah story?

DOUG   There's no huffing and puffing in the Noah story. Just one helluva storm.

KEITH   I want to be Noah. Without a script.

DOUG   Don't bail out on me, Keith. Not now.

KEITH   I want to be Noah next time.

DOUG   (*beat*) First things first, all right?

KEITH   I'll be a different Noah. My Noah will say "Yes". Yes to all the hippos. Yes to all the horses. Yes to all the giraffes. Yes, yes, yes, yes, yes, yes, yes,…

DOUG   (*cuts him off*) We have a show to put on.

KEITH   We'll do my show later. After the operation.

DOUG   After. So…. So let's ask ourselves what Tina needs today.

KEITH   Like a horoscope! It tells you what's going to happen. What you should do.

> *KEITH pulls a newspaper clipping out of his back pocket and scans it for TINA's horoscope.*

Here! Here's Tina's. She's a crab. "All your hard work will finally pay off. Expect a big pay day of a different sort when fortune sneaks up on you and takes you by surprise." (*beat*) Wanna hear yours?

DOUG   No. (*beat*) Why don't you try Sandra?

KEITH   She's a bull.

> *KEITH scans SANDRA's horoscope as he exits.*
>
> *TINA's breathing surfaces. DOUG looks over the script by a worktable before walking over to TINA.*

TINA   *Laboured and painful.*

DOUG   Hey, pumpkin. (*beat*) After this morning's rehearsal I started thinking about spicing up the script. You know, maybe add a bear wearing a snorkel and fins. (*beat*) A giraffe covered in sunscreen. (*beat*) Two sheep squabbling over a towel. (*beat*) That's what happens when you spend too much time with Keith. Anything goes. (*beat*) If Keith had his way, hippos would fly and we'd all be speaking hippo, too. The truth is, you don't have to speak hippo to do best by Hippo. (*beat*) Keith would say "Yes, yes, yes," to everyone and everything. But what does that get you? More of the same. (*beat*) Nothing changes. (*beat*) Things get worse. (*beat*) You—

SANDRA enters, stopping DOUG in his tracks. She's carrying a bag in one hand and holding an unbuttoned sweater tightly over her top with the other.

SANDRA   Don't let me interrupt.

DOUG   We were just chatting.

SANDRA   About?

DOUG   It's a father-daughter thing.

SANDRA   No room for a mother who should "shift lanes, slow down and share the road." (*beat*) Keith read me my horoscope this morning. (*beat*) And yours. And his. And Tina's. And on and on and on...

DOUG   I've told him a thousand times not to put too much faith in those things.

SANDRA   It's harmless.

DOUG   What's that you got there?

SANDRA   Something for you. (*to TINA*) And you, sweetheart. (*beat*) Close your eyes.

DOUG does as he's told. SANDRA takes off her sweater and reveals a custom-made hockey jersey. 'Team TINA' is stitched across the front, with a "C" on the left-hand side.

What'd'you think?

She models the sweatshirt for DOUG, who has opened his eyes.

DOUG   Looks great. (*beat*) What's Team Tina?

SANDRA   A small army of women that'll help out at the rehab centre.

DOUG   You plan on skating there?

SANDRA   It was Vera's idea. She's drawn up this whole schedule. She'll pitch in, of course. So will Darlene, Meg, Louise and Alexa. Elsie, her kids are gone now. She can fill in on short notice. That makes six of them. I thought of the name.

DOUG   Team Tina.

> *SANDRA shows DOUG his jersey.*

SANDRA   Yours has a 'C' on it, too. You know. Co-captains.

DOUG   Nice.

SANDRA   This one.... This one's for Tina.

> *SANDRA pulls another sweatshirt out of the bag and displays a beautiful but surprisingly small jersey bedecked with small jewels.*

Try yours on.

> *SANDRA tosses DOUG's jersey to him.*

DOUG   Not just now.

SANDRA   You don't like it?

DOUG   I like it just fine. You did a beautiful job.

> *SANDRA looks at the finished ark.*

SANDRA   That's a beautiful ark. You have a name for it yet?

DOUG   I'm working on it.

SANDRA   How's the play coming along?

DOUG   Keith is still wrestling with his lines, but he'll
           manage.

SANDRA   You fix a date for the show?

DOUG   You plan on selling tickets?

SANDRA   It helps me, knowing what's happening when. (*beat*)
           My heart jumps every time the phone rings, thinking
           it's Dr. Kovacs. I can't stand all this waiting. This not
           knowing.

DOUG   We know what Dr. Kovacs plans on doing. She made
           that perfectly clear.

SANDRA   We don't know how it'll turn out. That's out of our
           hands. So I started to think about what we can
           control. How a can-do attitude is a recipe for taking
           control.

DOUG   You're starting to sound like a horoscope.

SANDRA   I made two lists. Things to do before the operation,
           and things to bring.

           She pulls out her lists.

           (*to TINA*) We wouldn't dream of not bringing your
           nightlight, sweetheart. That's right at the top of the
           list.

DOUG   What's on your "To Do" list?

SANDRA   (*scans list*) Order flowers. Return library books. (*beat*)
           Church.

           DOUG shakes his head.

C'mon, Doug. You haven't been in almost a year.

DOUG Ever since they put those steel rods in her back.

SANDRA You.... You never told me that was why.

DOUG I never felt the need to explain.

SANDRA (*beat*) Until now.

DOUG They won't just be drilling this time. This, this '
salvage procedure'. You salvage cars, for Chrissake,
not kids. (*pause*) We didn't call her on it. Dr. Kovacs.
We sat there and listened and... and didn't challenge
her. We should have challenged her.

SANDRA We were in shock.

DOUG And now we're putting Tina's life into someone else's
hands again.

SANDRA Dr. Kovacs is one of the best. You've said so yourself.

DOUG She's not God.

SANDRA That's why we should both go to church. Make our
prayers twice as loud.

DOUG I'll take a raincheck.

SANDRA I thought if we both went. I don't know. Maybe
things will turn out all right.

DOUG Things have a way of sorting themselves out.

SANDRA That's God's job. To sort things out.

DOUG And we're supposed to stand back and watch him
sort?

SANDRA   What d'you want to do, Doug? Challenge him to
          a debate?

DOUG   Sometimes, God's gotta cut us a little slack.

SANDRA   Sometimes he does.

DOUG   Fine. The day God's ready to negotiate you let me
          know.

SANDRA   It doesn't work that way.

DOUG   How does it work, Sandra?

SANDRA   We're not alone in this. We're surrounded by good
          people.

          *SANDRA begins folding the hockey sweaters and
          putting them away.*

DOUG   Wearing the same sweater doesn't mean you've worn
          the same shoes. Vera, Elsie, Darlene. They don't know
          what we know.

TINA   *Jagged.*

DOUG   (*beat*) Tina's ours. We've been making choices for her
          from the moment she was born. When she eats. When
          she sleeps. When she shits. (*beat*) Why stop now?

SANDRA   We haven't stopped.

DOUG   We have. We're giving her up.

SANDRA   Don't talk that way. (*to TINA*) Everything will be for
          the best, sweetheart. (*to DOUG*) Team Tina.

DOUG   (*beat*) Team Tina.

          SANDRA exits. TINA's breathing fades.

DOUG begins to paint the ark. KEITH enters, wearing a Team TINA jersey with an "A" stitched on the left-hand side. He's carrying a square, hinged box with a different-coloured "T" on each side.

KEITH   Vera talks too much. Meg, too.

DOUG   Is that why you're here?

KEITH   (nods) Too much talking. Not enough brownies.

DOUG   Elsie brought two dozen.

KEITH   They were delicious.

DOUG   You ate two dozen brownies?

KEITH   They were small. (*beat*) Sandra kicked me out of the house. Sort of. She asked me to touch up Tina's T-box.

DOUG   Go ahead and touch up.

DOUG continues to paint. KEITH helps himself to what he needs. They paint in silence.

KEITH   This is nice. This is like when we go fishing. We don't talk.

DOUG   What's that supposed to mean?

KEITH   I like when we sit and sit and sit and it's like we're talking but we don't have to say anything.

DOUG   I hear you.

They resume painting.

KEITH   The hardware store, too.

DOUG   What about it?

KEITH   When we unload bags of sand. Bag after bag after bag. No talking. But it's like we're talking.

DOUG   (*beat*) Let's try some of that... no-talk talking now.

>   *The painting continues. KEITH breaks the silence when he starts to hum.*

Do you have to hum?

KEITH   We hum when we fish.

DOUG   We're not fishing.

KEITH   We can pretend we're fishing.

DOUG   We can pretend we're fishing but not humming.

KEITH   I like when you hum and then I hum with you. (*beat*) A duet.

DOUG   No duets today, okay?

KEITH   Soon?

DOUG   Soon.

KEITH   (*beat*) We can pretend it's soon and—

DOUG   Keith!

>   *They resume painting.*

KEITH   Why do fish travel in schools?

DOUG   Is this some kind of riddle?

KEITH   Why do we say "schools" for a bunch of fish and... and herds for a bunch of cows and... a... gaggle of geese?

DOUG   I didn't invent language, Keith.

            They paint in silence, but it's short-lived.

KEITH   How many cows do you need for a herd?

DOUG   Jesus, Keith.

KEITH   If it's say, thirty, does that mean twenty-nine cows are
            just a bunch of cows until another cow walks up and
            then all of a sudden they're a herd?

DOUG   Could be.

KEITH   Think how special that cow would feel.

DOUG   She's a cow, for Chrissake.

KEITH   Not to the other cows. Because of that one cow they
            go from being a "bunch" to a "herd".

            KEITH adds the final touches to the T-box.

            Done! (*beat*) Can we go fishing soon and do the
            no-talk talking?

DOUG   Sounds good.

            KEITH exits. DOUG returns to the ark.

            *Lights shift. SANDRA enters the shed, carrying
            a bottle of wine and two glasses.*

SANDRA   So, where're we going tonight?

DOUG   Didn't Gwen tell you?

SANDRA   She never had the chance. (*beat*) I was putting Tina to
            bed, brushing her hair, and I started to think about
            the rehab centre. These strangers, they're perfectly

nice people, I know, but to them Tina's still a job. An eight-hour shift. We can't be there all day, every day, day in, day out. (*beat*) Who's going to hum to her at night the way you do? Who's going to brush her hair first thing in the morning the way I do? Who's going to watch her watching birds? (*beat*) Then the doorbell rings and Gwen's at the door, holding this bottle of wine, telling me you've arranged for this night out and I just burst into tears. I'm still thinking of some stranger brushing Tina's hair. One stroke, two strokes and there they go, out the door. Poor Gwen didn't know what hit her and I couldn't explain. (*beat*) I am so tired. (*beat*) Tired, and ready to get plastered.

DOUG   Getting plastered isn't on the list.

> *DOUG pulls a list out of his pocket.*

I made a list of my own. Wine is number two. Number three is a baby sitter for three hours. Four is a movie. You gotta figure two hours for the movie and the drive into town. That leaves just under an hour for number one.

SANDRA   Which is?

> *DOUG grins.*

After I've had a few drinks.

DOUG   We're cutting it close.

SANDRA   We can make love later.

DOUG   Later's not the same. Later means Tina's in the next room.

SANDRA   So?

DOUG   So. So studies have shown that... that the closer you
            are to your kids' bedroom, the worse the sex.

SANDRA   (*laughs*) Studies have shown that parents of disabled
            kids are... are ten times more likely to have a drink-
            ing problem than parents of kids who... who can
            brush their own hair.

DOUG   Where did you read that?

SANDRA   I made it up. But I could believe it.

DOUG   You don't have a drinking problem.

SANDRA   I wish I did. (*beat*) I wish drinking was my only
            problem. (*beat*) I'm not making sense, am I?

DOUG   You're tired.

            DOUG massages SANDRA's neck.

SANDRA   (*grinning*) I'm not that tired.

            She turns and kisses DOUG. Lights fade.

            *TINA's breathing signals a shift in lighting, and
            marks her presence in the shed at the start of the
            puppet show. DOUG dons his Noah costume.
            SANDRA takes her place next to TINA.*

TINA   *Strained and shallow.*

DOUG   Sit back and prepare to be delighted and amazed. The
            story you're about to hear is an old story. Older than
            the hills. But just because it's old doesn't mean we
            can't learn something new. I hope you learn
            something today. (*beat*) Enjoy the show.

            *SANDRA applauds. KEITH enters, dressed in full
            Biblical garb, carrying a large basket of stuffed
            animals and an old-style megaphone.*

> Once upon a time there was a man named Noah. He was a simple man who led a simple life. One day he was tending his flock of sheep when he heard a voice.

KEITH   Baaaa!

DOUG   (*to KEITH*) Not the sheep. God.

KEITH   Oh, yeah. (*through megaphone*) Noah!

DOUG   Yes, God.

KEITH   When I look down and see what has happened, I don't like what I see.

DOUG   What do you see?

KEITH   Bad things. (*pause*) Corruption. Violence. (*beat*) Pain and suffering.

DOUG   What do you want me to do, Lord?

KEITH   You must build an ark.

DOUG   An ark?

KEITH   An ark.

DOUG   Then what?

KEITH   Bring one pair of everything. (*beat*) A pair of elephants. A pair of camels. A pair of giraffes. (*beat*) A pair of mitts.

**DOUG &
SANDRA**   Mitts?

KEITH   (*to TINA*) It will be cold on the ark.

DOUG   You want me to do the gathering?

KEITH   Yes.

DOUG   Why me, Lord?

KEITH   Who else, Noah? Your wife?

DOUG   No.

KEITH   Your sons?

DOUG   No. I will do it. (*beat*) When do I start?

KEITH   Soon.

DOUG   How soon?

KEITH   Now soon. Prepare for a storm to end all storms.

DOUG   Shem!

KEITH   (*still God-like*) Yes, father. (*puts megaphone down*) Yes, father.

DOUG   Shem, is the ramp ready?

> *KEITH darts over to the shed wall where the ramp leans.*

KEITH   Yes, father.

DOUG   Come, my son. There is work to be done.

> *KEITH places the ramp so it leads onto the ark.*

Listen. Do you hear the distant thunder?

KEITH   No.

DOUG   Is that not thunder you hear?

KEITH   Yes! Thunder.

> *KEITH grabs a small piece of sheet metal and bangs it to make the sound of thunder.*

Loud thunder.

DOUG   It is God's warning. A violent storm will soon be upon us.

KEITH   (*pause*) Wait!

> *KEITH runs to his basket and picks up the jar DOUG gave him. It's filled with water and capped with a lid punctured with holes. KEITH turns the jar over and sprinkles water across the stage.*

It rained and rained and rained and rained and rained and rained…

DOUG   That's enough rain, Keith.

KEITH   … and rained and rained and rained…

DOUG   Cut the rain, Keith.

> *KEITH stops sprinkling water.*

KEITH   It rained for forty days.

DOUG   We don't have forty days. We have a show to put on. (*reverts to Noah role*) Here is the list. Let us begin.

KEITH   Yes, father.

> *KEITH puts the jar down. DOUG unrolls a scroll.*

DOUG   Horses.

> *KEITH picks up two stuffed horses from the basket.*

KEITH   Horses.

> *KEITH makes the appropriate animal noises as DOUG ticks off the list. KEITH makes it a point to entertain TINA as he pushes the horses up the ramp and places them on deck.*

DOUG   Pigs.

> *KEITH plucks two stuffed pigs from the basket.*

KEITH   Pigs.

> *DOUG checks off the list. KEITH imitates pigs, eyeing TINA as he pushes the pigs up the ramp. This pattern continues throughout the following sequence, which quickly devolves into comic mayhem as KEITH struggles to keep up and ends up tossing the animals on board.*

DOUG   Donkeys.

KEITH   Donkeys.

DOUG   Monkeys.

KEITH   Monkeys.

DOUG   Quickly, Shem. The rain is falling. (*beat*) Cows.

KEITH   Cows.

DOUG   Sheep.

KEITH   Sheep.

DOUG   Quickly!

KEITH   Quickly.

DOUG   Pull up the ramp. God has spoken.

KEITH   We're not finished.

DOUG   It's too late.

KEITH   Don't forget Hippo.

> *KEITH flings a stuffed hippo onto the ark.*

DOUG   (*low*) I told you. I took out the hippo scene.

KEITH   (*ignores DOUG*) And Hippo's brother.

> *KEITH tosses another hippo.*

DOUG   We don't have time for this.

KEITH   (*beat*) And his sister.

> *KEITH tosses one more hippo onto the ark.*

DOUG   There's no room, Keith!

KEITH   Shem.

DOUG   Shem.

KEITH   We can make room. (*beat*) We can make room for Hippo's mother and father.

> *KEITH tosses two more hippos.*

DOUG   I told you. Not everyone can get on.

KEITH   Hippo's cousin.

> *Another hippo sails through the air.*

DOUG   Stop!

> *KEITH pays no heed and tosses the rest of the hippo clan onto the ark with abandon. DOUG tries catching them. TINA's breath becomes erratic.*

KEITH   Make room for a bunch of happy hippos!

> *TINA's breathing becomes jagged.*

SANDRA   Oh, shit. Here we go...

DOUG   *(to KEITH)* We've done what we can!

KEITH   Seizure! Seizure, seizure, seizure.

TINA   *Very frantic.*

SANDRA   It's okay, sweetheart.

DOUG   Easy, Tina.

KEITH   I can hum. She likes it when I hum.

SANDRA   Hum, Keith.

> *KEITH starts to hum.*

KEITH   The humming's not working.

DOUG   Just wait it out.

KEITH   The humming helps. Usually.

> *KEITH resumes humming, to no avail.*

SANDRA   We're with you, sweetheart.

KEITH   Make it work! Make the humming work!

> *TINA's seizure intensifies.*

SANDRA   Easy, Tina. Ease up.

KEITH   It's not working!

>   *Distraught beyond words, KEITH bolts for the shed door.*

DOUG   Keith, it's not your fault. (*beat*) Keith!

SANDRA   It's okay, Tina. It's okay.

>   *DOUG and SANDRA continue to soothe TINA. Her breathing slowly subsides.*
>
>   *DOUG and SANDRA wait and watch. TINA eases into a steady rhythm.*

(*pause*) When I think of the operation, know what I think about?

DOUG   You know what I hear? (*beat*) A saw. You have any idea what this saw looks like?

SANDRA   No.

DOUG   Me, neither. But I can hear it. I can't help hearing it. The sound of that saw cutting through her bone, I tell you, it keeps me up at night.

SANDRA   I don't get that far.

DOUG   What'd'you mean?

SANDRA   There's no saw. No rehab. (*beat*) No operation.

DOUG   What are you getting at?

SANDRA   Some nurse takes pity on her and, and does whatever it is they do and Tina sleeps. (*pause*) She falls asleep and never wakes up.

DOUG   Like in a fairy tale.

SANDRA   No. In a fairy tale she wakes up. Some dashing prince comes by and gives her a princely kiss and she wakes up. (*beat*) Tina doesn't have a prince.

DOUG   What about us?

SANDRA   You have some magic wand I don't know about?

DOUG   No magic wand.

SANDRA   No. Just a saw.

DOUG   That's the trouble with Dr. Kovacs. She can't see outside the box.

SANDRA   There's nothing outside the box, Doug.

DOUG   Maybe there is.

SANDRA   We've tried everything. (*beat*) That herbal cocktail you ordered didn't help.

DOUG   Herbal remedies are in the box. Therapeutic massage? In the box. (*beat*) We have to step outside the box and do what's best for Tina. Isn't that what you want?

SANDRA   It's what I've always wanted.

DOUG   And you still think this operation is the answer?

SANDRA   (*pause*) It's all we have.

> As TINA's breathing fades SANDRA walks back to the house.
>
> DOUG picks up a long length of rubber hose. He lays it across his worktable and grabs a knife. KEITH stands by the doorway and watches. DOUG looks at the hose as if he half-expects it to speak.

KEITH   Is Tina okay?

DOUG   Christ, you scared me.

KEITH   I didn't want to bother you. You looked real busy.

DOUG   How long have you been standing there?

KEITH   I don't know.

DOUG   Look it, I have some work to do.

KEITH   Can we do it again? The puppet show. We didn't finish it. (*beat*) She didn't laugh.

DOUG   We tried, didn't we?

KEITH   We can try again.

DOUG   We'll see.

KEITH   Is it okay if I take some varnish? For my dove.

DOUG   Take whatever you need and go.

KEITH   What's the hose for?

DOUG   (*pause*) What does someone use a hose for?

KEITH   For watering.

DOUG   Well, that's what it's for. For watering.

KEITH   For the play! Instead of the bottle. We'll need lots of water, because it rained for forty days and forty nights. (*grins*) It rained and rained and rained and rained—

DOUG   Don't you get started.

KEITH	Forty days is a lot of rain.
DOUG	(*pause*) Think you could do it? You think you could stand forty days of rain?
KEITH	If I had my raincoat.
DOUG	No. No raincoat. Nothing to protect you.
KEITH	You're naked?
DOUG	From the moment you're born all you know is rain. Blinding rain. Sharp as nails.
KEITH	For forty days?
DOUG	Forever.
KEITH	That's why I need varnish. For protection.

> *KEITH grabs some varnish and leaves.*

DOUG   (*pause*) Wait!

> *KEITH steps back inside the shed.*

Grab that rope.

> *KEITH picks up a long rope.*

I need your help with something.

> *DOUG sits down on a chair and motions for KEITH to approach.*

Start with my hands.

KEITH   Why?

DOUG   Tie them.

KEITH doesn't move.

Tie my hands.

KEITH hesitates, then begins tying DOUG's hands.

Tighter. (*beat*) Tighter than that, Keith.

A frightened KEITH obliges.

Now work the rope around my head, keeping it good and tight. (*beat*) C'mon, Keith.

KEITH does as he's told.

You can do better than that. (*winces*) That's it. Now pull down. (*beat*) Pull.

DOUG's head is forced down, into his chest.

Good. (*beat*) Loop it around my legs. Keep looping until I say stop.

KEITH loops and pulls. Before long, DOUG is in obvious pain and discomfort.

Stop. (*beat*) Make a tight knot. (*beat*) Give it your best sailor's knot.

KEITH complies, then steps back.

Knock me over.

KEITH doesn't move.

Knock me over!

KEITH kicks the chair over. DOUG topples to the floor.

Come back in two hours. Do you understand?

KEITH   No.

DOUG   Just come back, okay? Two hours from now.

> *KEITH looks at DOUG.*

Okay?

KEITH   Okay.

> *KEITH stays rooted to the spot.*

DOUG   Go.

> *KEITH doesn't move.*

Go!

> *KEITH bolts out of the shed. DOUG's breathing is strained and desperate as he struggles for air. Lights fade, underscoring DOUG's laboured breaths.*
>
> *Lights up on SANDRA, cutting the rope binding DOUG.*

SANDRA   What the hell happened?

> *DOUG slowly gets to his feet.*

DOUG   It's hard to explain.

SANDRA   Try me.

DOUG   This wasn't Keith's doing. It was mine.

SANDRA   You asked him to hog-tie you?

DOUG   Pretty much.

SANDRA Why? (*pause*) You can't know what it's like. None of us can.

DOUG Doesn't mean you can't try.

SANDRA And then what? What do you do after your legs seize up and you can't feel your toes?

DOUG (*beat*) Then you cut out my tongue.

SANDRA Jesus, Doug. Don't talk that way.

DOUG Cut out my tongue so I can't speak. (*beat*) Twist my muscles into impossible knots. Twist them the way I've seen you wring a mop. Real tight. (*beat*) Drill holes into my back. Drill like my back was a sheet of plywood. If you hit a nerve, keep drilling, like you're drilling for oil, like you're drilling your way to the ends of the earth and won't stop until you get there. (*beat*) Saw off my thighbone. Saw it right off. Take the sawed off part and shove it back into the hip socket. It won't fit, right, 'cause you've sawed off the ball part. C'mon. Shove that cut-off bone into the socket where it belongs. (*beat*) Stick a feeding tube into me. You heard what Kovacs said. Chances are good I'm going to lose even more weight. Thirty-eight pounds and dropping. Get that feeding tube into me. A tube for every hole in my body while you're at it.

SANDRA Stop it.

DOUG It won't stop. You heard Kovacs. It will not stop. More operations. More 'intervention'. (*beat*) When you're finished. When you've finished all your cutting and drilling and sawing, send in my parents. My parents, they love me. God, yes. Their love, it's like my daily seizures. It's a sure thing. Thing is, it's not enough. (*beat*) My pain is greater than my parent's love. (*beat*) No more. (*beat*) No more.

> *SANDRA walks over and places her hand on DOUG.*

SANDRA Dr. Kovacs phoned. That's why I came running here. (*beat*) It's all set. Next Tuesday at eleven. (*pause*) I'm going to fix you a drink.

> *DOUG is motionless. SANDRA exits through the shed door.*
>
> *TINA's breathing surfaces. Lights shift.*
>
> *DOUG eavesdrops on the conversation outside the shed. TINA is in her usual spot.*

TINA *Even but forceful.*

SANDRA (*off stage*) Why are you standing out here?

KEITH (*off stage*) 'Cause.

SANDRA 'Cause why?

KEITH 'Cause I want to. (*beat*) You look nice.

SANDRA Thank you.

KEITH Where're you going?

SANDRA I'm off to church. (*beat*) It's warmer inside.

KEITH I want to stay here. For now.

SANDRA (*beat*) Don't go blaming yourself for what happened last night, Keith.

KEITH What happened?

SANDRA Speak to Doug. (*beat*) See you later.

> *DOUG listens attentively for the sound of*

*DOUG listens attentively for the sound of
SANDRA driving off. KEITH enters but stops at
the doorway, unable to contain his nervous energy.*

DOUG   I won't bite.

KEITH stays huddled by the doorway.

Close the door, will ya.

*KEITH takes a step forward and closes the door
behind him. He sends a small, self-conscious wave
to TINA.*

Cat got your tongue?

KEITH shakes his head.

KEITH   (*pause*) Are you okay?

DOUG   I'm fine. You look all wired up.

KEITH   (*pause*) You weren't here last night. I came back, like
you told me to. I came back after two hours. (*beat*)
You weren't here.

DOUG curses to himself silently.

DOUG   I'm sorry.

KEITH   I'm sorry. For hurting you. (*pause*) Don't make me
hurt you again. Please.

DOUG   I won't.

KEITH   I was scared. When I came back and saw you were
gone. I was scared something happened to you.

DOUG   I'm fine.

KEITH   (*beat*) I need it back. My dove. I forgot it here last night.

> *KEITH stops by the (unseen) truck on his way to get the dove.*

Why's the truck in here?

DOUG   Needs a tune up.

KEITH   Can I help?

DOUG   No. I've got lots to do today, Keith.

KEITH   I've got lots to do today, too, Doug. Wanna hint?

> *DOUG doesn't reply.*

Okay. Hint number one. (*beat*) Everyone has them.

> *DOUG can't play along.*

They come in pairs. (*beat*) Mine aren't real.

DOUG   I give up.

KEITH   The eyes! The eyes for the dove are here. Crenshaw's called and left a message. They're here. (*to TINA*) I'm happy for you.

DOUG   I'm happy for you. Why don't you bike down and pick 'em up?

KEITH   Crenshaw's doesn't open 'til noon on Sundays.

DOUG   (*pause*) You know those horoscopes you love?

KEITH   I haven't read them today. Not yet.

DOUG   You got plenty of time. Tell you what.

DOUG pulls a bill out of his pocket and hands it to KEITH.

Here's twenty bucks. You hunt down all the horoscopes you can find. Those astrology magazines I've seen at the supermarket.

KEITH   And the little ones you can buy, all rolled up in tiny tubes. A different colour for every month.

DOUG   You buy as many different horoscopes as you can. Get yourself a booth at Clancy's, order a big drink and then compare 'em.

KEITH   The price?

DOUG   Not the price. The... the predictions. Whatever you call 'em. Take a... a Capricorn from one of those tiny tube horoscopes and compare it with a Capricorn from a magazine. See what you come up with. See if they say the same thing.

KEITH   I'll start with yours.

DOUG   Start with yours.

KEITH   Then yours.

DOUG   If there's time.

KEITH   Then Tina's.

DOUG   You better get going. You won't get through half the zodiac signs before Crenshaw's opens.

KEITH steps out the door. He returns a moment later to talk to TINA wearing a playful grin.

KEITH   (*loud whisper*) I'll do yours first.

DOUG   Off you go.

> *DOUG shoos KEITH out the door. DOUG stands*
> *by the shed door to ensure KEITH leaves, then*
> *waves goodbye. He walks back to TINA.*

TINA   *Laboured but full of longing.*

DOUG   Hey, pumpkin. (*pause*) It's time to go. (*beat*) After
you're all settled in you'll start to feel sleepy. Like....
Like you're floating. Just like a bird. (*beat*) Just like
Keith's dove. (*beat*) The dove on Noah's ark, she finds
an olive branch. That's a good sign. It means the
floodwaters, they're dropping. A week later, Noah
sends the dove out again, only this time, the dove
doesn't come back. She finds a place to rest. (*pause*)
That's what it'll be like for you, sweetheart. Just like
that dove. I'll set you free, and... and you'll find a
place. (*pause*) I love you.

> *DOUG begins to hum a lullaby. As the lights fade,*
> *DOUG's lullaby blends with TINA's breathing.*

> *The braided sounds and dark stage are punctured by*
> *a car ignition and the bright headlights of DOUG's*
> *pickup. DOUG stands in the glare of the headlights,*
> *facing TINA in the cab of the pickup. DOUG stops*
> *humming. TINA stops breathing. The engine*
> *rumbles. Blackout. Silence.*

> *Lights up. DOUG sits crouched by the ark. KEITH*
> *enters, holding the dove behind his back. He stands*
> *in front of DOUG, eager for his attention.*

KEITH   Look! I finished it. I glued on the eyes. See?

> *DOUG looks up at KEITH's dove.*

They don't look real but she won't mind. (*beat*) You
think she'll mind if the dove's eyes don't look real?

DOUG tries to make sense of the moment.

Can I show it to her? (*beat*) The dove. Can I show it to
Tina?

DOUG   What?

KEITH   We can finish the Noah play. The dove is ready to fly
away and never come back. That's what you wrote.
That's how it ends.

DOUG   No.

KEITH   I have to practice. The dove couldn't fly before 'cause
it didn't have eyes. Now it can see. (*beat*) "Shem,
release the dove." "Yes, father."

> *KEITH waltzes around the stage, moving the dove
> as if it was soaring above the seas, singing as
> though he was the jubilant dove itself.*

(*as the dove*) Hang on, Tina!

DOUG   What are you doing?

KEITH   I'm the dove. Tina's on my back.

DOUG   That's enough, Keith.

KEITH   I haven't finished.

DOUG   Now is not a good time.

KEITH   When?

DOUG   Leave the dove with me for now.

KEITH   We can hang it up. With the others. We can surprise
Tina. We'll bring her in and shout, "Surprise!" (*beat*)
I love surprises.

DOUG   Leave it with me. (*beat*) Please.

>   *DOUG takes the dove. KEITH exits.*

KEITH   (*off stage*) He's grumpy today.

SANDRA   (*off stage*) So am I.

>   *SANDRA enters, dressed in the outfit she wore to church.*

Why aren't you in the house with Tina?

DOUG   (*pause*) She's sleeping.

SANDRA   I know.

DOUG   (*beat*) You know?

SANDRA   I poked my head into her room. When did she fall asleep?

DOUG   About an hour ago.

SANDRA   Tell me you haven't been here since then. God knows what could have happened.

DOUG   What did she look like? When you saw her?

SANDRA   Peaceful. And alone.

>   *SANDRA turns and heads for the shed door.*

DOUG   Wait.

SANDRA   I don't want to wait. I have to wake her up.

DOUG   Now?

SANDRA   She's gotta eat.

DOUG   I'm not hungry.

SANDRA   Are you okay?

DOUG   How was church?

SANDRA   We'll have to wait and see.

DOUG   What does that mean?

SANDRA   I said my prayers. Now I hope they're answered.

             SANDRA continues toward the shed door.

DOUG   Don't. (*beat*) Don't go in without me.

SANDRA   I know my way to the house, Doug.

DOUG   You.... You don't know the whole story.

SANDRA   What story? (*beat*) What are you talking about?

DOUG   Tina.

SANDRA   What about her?

DOUG   (*pause*) She's so peaceful when she sleeps.

SANDRA   (*edgy*) Very peaceful. (*beat*) Can I go now?

             *SANDRA is about to open the shed door when
             DOUG calls out.*

DOUG   She deserves peace!

             *SANDRA stops in her tracks and turns to face
             DOUG.*

Peace of mind. Peace of body. She's entitled to that.
(*pause*) Everlasting peace.

*An unbearable silence blankets the shed. Frozen to
the spot, SANDRA finally turns around and runs
out the shed door.*

Wait. (*beat*) Wait for me. (*beat*) Sandra!

*DOUG runs to the shed door, then stops. He
doesn't give chase. He sits and awaits SANDRA's
return. The long silence that envelops DOUG is
fractured by SANDRA's arrival at the shed door.
She stands there, wordlessly. DOUG moves toward
her. He makes a motion to embrace her, then
reconsiders. He waits for SANDRA to make the
next move. She stares at him, then slaps DOUG
with a suddenness that stuns. She explodes with
a fury that leaves DOUG paralysed. She pummels
him with her fists, relentless in her rage. Finally,
SANDRA stops, exhausted. Lights fade.*

*The sound of a siren slowly surfaces off-stage, then
fades. Lights up on the empty shed. KEITH, dressed
in his funeral suit, enters the shed. He grabs a pair
of shears. KEITH positions himself beneath one of
the marionettes dangling from the rafters and snips
the cords holding it in place. It crashes to the floor.
He cuts down several more. DOUG enters.*

DOUG   You think that's what Tina wants?

KEITH   Tina's dead.

DOUG   Doesn't mean we have to pretend she was never here.

KEITH   I'm not pretending.

DOUG   Cutting those puppets down, what's the good in that?

KEITH   No more puppet shows. (*beat*) No more Tina.

DOUG   Tina's still here.

KEITH   Where?

DOUG   In you. In me. When someone dies we carry a piece of them with us.

KEITH   I don't want a piece of Tina. I want Tina.

DOUG   She can't come back, Keith.

KEITH   I miss her.

DOUG   Me, too.

KEITH   The puppets make me miss her more.

> *DOUG watches as KEITH cuts down the puppets. The sound as they hit the floor is too much to bear.*

DOUG   Stop it.

KEITH   I'm not finished.

> *KEITH continues cutting down the puppets until not a single one remains. He gathers them in a pile where TINA used to sit.*

DOUG   Now what?

KEITH   (*pause*) We should bury them.

DOUG   One burial was enough. Don't you think?

KEITH   The puppets were her friends. They want to be with her.

DOUG   They're puppets, Keith. You don't bury puppets.

KEITH   Why not?

DOUG   They were never alive. You bury hamsters. Goldfish, maybe. Not puppets.

KEITH   They made her laugh.

DOUG   They did.

KEITH   They had names.

DOUG   I know.

KEITH   It's like they were real.

DOUG   They're still puppets.

KEITH   Tina's puppets. (*beat*) They should be with Tina.

DOUG   You can't bury them next to Tina.

KEITH   We can bury them here. A little puppet cemetery.

DOUG   No.

KEITH   Why not?

DOUG   I don't want to spend my days walking around puppet tombstones.

KEITH   Tina would like that.

DOUG   You don't know that.

KEITH   How do you know she wouldn't?

DOUG   (*beat*) I'll tell you what she'd like. (*beat*) I'll tell you what we'll do. Let's hang up that dove of yours. That's how you want to remember Tina. Not in the ground but high in the air.

KEITH   Did she like it? Did she like the eyes?

DOUG   (*pause*) She loved it. (*beat*) Tell you what. Get the
ladder and we'll hang it up right now.

> *DOUG gets the mourning dove from where it was
> left. KEITH brings over a stepladder. DOUG gives
> him the dove to hold as he mounts the ladder.*

Hand me that beautiful dove of yours.

> *KEITH hands him the dove.*

KEITH   Careful.

DOUG   You bet.

> *DOUG attaches the dove to some strings that once
> held another puppet. The dove hangs alone amongst
> the rafters.*

Isn't that a sight to behold?

KEITH   (*pause*) I love you. (*beat*) That's what my horoscope
said to do. The one I bought with the money you
gave me. "Love's labour's lost can be found with
a bit of digging. Find a moment to tell someone close
to you how you feel." (*beat*) I love you. (*beat*) How do
you feel?

DOUG   (*pause*) Hard to say.

> *DOUG climbs down the ladder and puts it away.
> He surveys the fallen marionettes. He hesitates,
> then takes the handle of a large, colourful child's
> wagon, customized to accommodate TINA. He and
> KEITH pick up the puppets as though gathering the
> dead, and place them in the wagon. When the floor
> has been cleared DOUG parks the wagon by a wall.
> He and KEITH stare at the wagon, as though
> standing vigil. Lights fade. KEITH exits.*

> *SANDRA enters, no longer dressed for church,
> carrying a laundry basket filled with DOUG's
> clothes, topped with a blanket, thermos and lunch
> pail.*

> *SANDRA folds the clothes and hands them to
> DOUG, who arranges them in piles on the
> worktable.*

SANDRA How long are you planning on staying here?

DOUG I don't know.

SANDRA The mattress holding up?

DOUG No complaints.

SANDRA I brought you an extra blanket.

> *They continue to fold and sort the clothes, turning
> the mundane into the meditative.*

We should have waited.

DOUG Waited for what, Sandra? (*beat*) A sign? (*beat*) Waited
for God to whisper into your ear while you were
praying in church?

SANDRA This has nothing to do with God, and everything to
do with you. (*beat*) You and me and Tina.

DOUG That's how it's always been. The three of us.

SANDRA The three of us weren't there. (*pause*) How long did
you stay with her?

DOUG Don't do this to yourself.

SANDRA I'm doing it for Tina. (*beat*) How did you know? (*beat*)
How did you know when it was time to go?

DOUG   It's not something I timed, Sandra. I just knew it was time.

SANDRA   You strapped her in?

DOUG   I put a towel around her neck. To make her more comfortable.

SANDRA   She looked comfortable?

DOUG   Yes.

SANDRA   Were you close enough to hear her?

DOUG   I was close by. (*beat*) She didn't cry. If she had cried I would have gone back for her. She never cried. (*beat*) It was painless.

SANDRA   You don't know that. You don't know she didn't cry because you weren't by her side to the very end. You couldn't stay to the very end. (*beat*) You stepped out of the truck. You left her alone. (*beat*) Where was I?

DOUG   You were in church.

SANDRA   No. I mean, where was I? Where was I when you strapped her in, when you made sure she was comfortable, when you turned on the ignition? Did you have any last minute conversations with me? (*pause*) You said, "I love you." Those were your last words.

DOUG   Yes.

SANDRA   Why didn't you say, "We love you"? (*pause*) Maybe you didn't speak for me because you hadn't spoken to me. Maybe you were deathly afraid I would say no.

DOUG   We don't have to speak in order to be heard.

SANDRA (*pause*) Maybe if I hadn't wanted it so badly.

DOUG That's guilty talk. You're not guilty. Neither am I.

SANDRA What are we then? Now that she's gone.

DOUG Her parents. That doesn't end, does it?

SANDRA I don't feel like much of a parent right now.

DOUG You wanted it to end.

SANDRA Yes. (*beat*) I never said I wanted you to end it.

DOUG You wanted some nurse to have mercy on her. You wanted someone else to take responsibility because you couldn't do it yourself.

SANDRA Not couldn't. Wouldn't. (*pause*) I've come close, though.

DOUG When?

SANDRA (*pause*) A year ago, maybe. Not long after she'd had the steel rods put in. She'd just had a seizure and was drifting to sleep. She looked so peaceful. That got me thinking about what it's like when she's awake. It's the opposite of peace. It's war. (*beat*) It's like she's been fighting this war since the day she was born. Imagine battling your own body.

DOUG I've tried.

SANDRA How much could she endure? This… this steady assault. I wanted it to end. (*pause*) I wanted to end it. I wanted her to sleep and sleep and keep sleeping because when she sleeps there's no pain. I took one of her pillows and… and I held it. I held it for a very long time. I lifted the pillow up. I brought it toward her face. Then I looked at Tina. Our Tina. I saw…

I could see how I was holding the pillow. It wasn't a pillow anymore. I had my hands… I was holding it like a shield. Like I was shielding her from something. Or someone. I looked at this pillow, this shield, and knew I had no choice. I knew I had to protect her, no matter what the cost. (*beat*) I lay down beside her, lay my head on the pillow and held her close.

DOUG   You never told me.

SANDRA   I was afraid of what you'd think of me.

DOUG   (*pause*) Now I know what you think of me.

SANDRA   (*pause*) You were trying to protect her. (*beat*) You were trying to protect me.

DOUG   I wanted you to keep your hands clean.

SANDRA   (*beat*) These hands once clutched a pillow for the longest time. (*pause*) You think Mrs. Noah and her husband talked things over?

DOUG   I don't know.

SANDRA   She might have told him to leave God's work to God. (*beat*) She might have convinced him that drowning the blameless is a bad start. (*pause*) Maybe…. Maybe she'd snuck a peek at the Promised Land and saw it was full of broken promises. (*beat*) My hunch is Noah told Mrs. Noah they were taking a long trip and skimped on the details.

DOUG   I'd have to brush up on my Bible.

SANDRA   You're not the Bible-brushing type, Doug. (*beat*) You've always had faith in yourself.

DOUG   (*pause*) And in you.

SANDRA   (*beat*) And Keith expects you to open the store on time. Off you go.

> DOUG *grabs the thermos and lunch pail and exits.*
>
> *Lights shift.* KEITH *enters the shed, dressed in a casual outfit, as* SANDRA *folds* DOUG'*s mattress and bedding.*

KEITH   He yelled at me.

SANDRA   I heard.

KEITH   That's the job of a judge? To yell at people?

SANDRA   You kept pushing his buttons.

KEITH   He wouldn't let me speak.

SANDRA   It's his courtroom.

KEITH   Doug is my friend.

SANDRA   You made that perfectly clear.

KEITH   He didn't let me finish. (*imitating judge*) "Young man, you're out of line."

SANDRA   What would you have said? If he had let you finish?

KEITH   I'd tell him Dougie would never hurt Tina. He loved her too much.

SANDRA   You can hurt people you love, Keith.

KEITH   Tina's not hurt. She's dead. (*pause*) Some people talk crazy talk.

SANDRA   Which people?

KEITH   Crazy people.

SANDRA   What are these crazy people saying?

KEITH   Crazy talk.

SANDRA   About Doug?

KEITH   Crazy talk about Doug and a hose. (*beat*) Doug and Tina and a hose. Crazy, eh?

> *SANDRA doesn't respond.*

Hoses are for watering.

> *KEITH searches for the hose.*

Where's the hose?

SANDRA   They took it away. It's evidence, now.

KEITH   It's not evidence. It's a hose. He has to tell them. Doug has to tell them hoses are for watering. Then all the crazy talk will stop.

SANDRA   It won't stop, Keith.

KEITH   Why not?

SANDRA   Being charged is just the beginning.

KEITH   He should be uncharged.

SANDRA   He'll be out on bail real soon.

KEITH   (*beat*) There's no crazy talk about you.

SANDRA   People are talking about me.

KEITH   Why?

SANDRA   (*pause*) They're wondering where I was in all this.

KEITH   You were in church. When Tina died in her sleep you were in church. (*beat*) You feel bad about that.

SANDRA   Yes.

KEITH   I bet she looked beautiful. I bet she looked beautiful when she died in her sleep 'cause you brushed her hair. Every night. Before she fell asleep.

SANDRA   Not this time. (*beat*) Only Doug.

KEITH   Did he hum to her?

> *SANDRA nods.*

I knew it! (*beat*) Tell the judge. Tell the judge Doug hummed her to sleep. No hoses. Humming.

> *KEITH begins to hum the same lullaby DOUG hummed as she sat in the truck.*

(*imitating judge*) "There'll be no humming in this court, young man. Is that understood?"

> *KEITH ignores the judge.*

(*as judge*) Did you hear me?

> *KEITH defies the judge and continues to hum the lullaby.*

(*as judge*) I said no humming!

> *KEITH steps up the humming.*

(*as judge*) Humming is strictly forbidden.

> *KEITH hums even more aggressively… and enjoys it.*

(*as judge*) Stop it!

> *KEITH is into in-your-face humming. SANDRA can't contain her laughter.*

SANDRA   (*laughing*) Stop! Stop it!

KEITH   He's a lousy judge.

SANDRA   And I'm a lousy mother. (*beat*) That's what people are saying, Keith. I'm a God-awful mother to have let this happen.

KEITH   You weren't there.

SANDRA   That's the half of it. They can't understand how I can live under the same roof as Doug. (*beat*) I have to tell you, some days I'm tempted to leave.

KEITH   Where would you go?

SANDRA   Anywhere.

KEITH   You can't go. Make them understand.

SANDRA   I can't make anyone understand Doug.

KEITH   I don't always understand Doug. (*pause*) Why he made me tie him up.

SANDRA   He was trying to understand what Tina was feeling.

KEITH   Tina wasn't tied up.

SANDRA   Tina was in pain.

KEITH   You don't have to be tied up to feel pain.

SANDRA No, you don't. (*beat*) I'm sorry you saw a side to Doug you'd never seen before. (*pause*) No. I'm not sorry. You should see him for who he is.

KEITH (*beat*) Who is he?

SANDRA Not the monster some people make him out to be.

KEITH Dougie's not a monster.

SANDRA No.

KEITH (*beat*) You're not a God-awful mother.

> *SANDRA shakes her head.*

Tell them. The people who talk crazy talk. Tell them who you and Dougie are so the crazy talk will stop.

> *SANDRA nods. KEITH exits. The lights shift.*

> *KEITH can be heard using an electric sander against one of the shed walls.*

> *SANDRA walks to the wagon filled with the cut marionettes.*

DOUG (*off-stage*) How much longer?

> *The sanding continues. SANDRA searches for a covering.*

(*louder*) How much longer are you gonna be?!

> *The sanding continues for a moment longer, then grinds to a halt. SANDRA takes the spare blanket she brought for DOUG and covers the marionettes.*

KEITH (*off-stage*) All done.

DOUG   (*off-stage*) You're not done.

KEITH   (*off-stage*) I am. I sanded it all off.

>   *KEITH enters. DOUG follows, carrying a large bag of mail.*

DOUG   They'll be back. (*beat*) Maybe next time they'll spell 'slaughterhouse' right.

KEITH   Whatever they write, I'll make it disappear.

SANDRA   More mail?

KEITH   See? He's famous.

DOUG   Not everyone's a fan, Keith. That graffiti you sanded off is—

KEITH   There'll be more. I know.

>   *KEITH digs into his pocket and pulls out a newspaper clipping.*

Did you see the picture of Dougie? In the newspaper?

SANDRA   I saw it.

>   *KEITH unfolds the clipping and shows it to SANDRA.*

KEITH   He's famous.

SANDRA   I don't know about that.

KEITH   He's important. (*beat*) More important than a horoscope. Horoscopes are always at the back. Not Dougie. He's on the front page. (*beat*) You never see horoscopes on the front page. Ever.

SANDRA   This isn't about horoscopes, Keith.

KEITH   I know.

SANDRA   Some people are saying some terrible things.

KEITH   Crazy people.

SANDRA   The crown attorney. He's making Doug out to be some kind of villain. It's all there on the front page. Doug Ramsay, the heartless father. Doug Ramsay, the pathetic parent who couldn't hack the hardship of life with a disabled daughter so he killed her. Doug Ramsay, the——

DOUG   Fuck him!

KEITH   You shouldn't swear.

DOUG   (*pause*) I'm sorry.

SANDRA   I want to testify. Barclay thinks it's a good idea, especially since you won't.

DOUG   Lawyers know best.

SANDRA   It's the crown attorney that worries me.

KEITH   I don't like his teeth.

SANDRA   The way he twists things.

KEITH   They're crooked.

DOUG   Don't say anything he can twist.

KEITH   He looks like a beaver.

SANDRA   I can't help what he does with my words.

KEITH   A beaver with ugly glasses.

DOUG   What are you going to say about me?

KEITH   You have to tell the truth, the whole truth, and nothing but the truth.

SANDRA   (*pause*) I'll tell them you loved her.

KEITH   I loved her, too.

SANDRA   We all do, Keith.

KEITH   Tell them what Doug is really like. "You, Sir, are courageous." That's what someone wrote. In a letter.

SANDRA   Did they say why?

KEITH   I just read the part Dougie showed me. "You, Sir, are courageous." I like that. "Sir".

DOUG   What will you tell them? (*beat*) About me and Tina?

KEITH   Tell them how Dougie took Tina out for Halloween.

SANDRA   You always did what was best for Tina.

KEITH   Always.

SANDRA   (*beat*) What you believed was best.

DOUG   And when they ask you what you believe? (*beat*) "Do you believe your husband did the right thing, Mrs. Ramsay? Under the circumstances."

> *SANDRA doesn't reply.*

KEITH   What circumstances?

DOUG   "Did he do the right thing, Mrs. Ramsay?"

SANDRA   (*pause*) Tina deserves.... Her death deserves to be
           understood.

KEITH   She died in her sleep.

SANDRA   I can explain her life. You explain her death.

DOUG   I have nothing to say to a judge or jury.

SANDRA   You expect me to talk for you?

DOUG   No. (*pause*) You don't like what people are saying, is
           that it? You want to set the record straight?

SANDRA   I've been spat on twice.

KEITH   Who?!

SANDRA   I've also been hugged by complete strangers.

KEITH   Why?

SANDRA   If no one speaks for Tina then it's like she's died
           a second time. (*beat*) I'm going to testify.

DOUG   They'll push you, Sandra. They'll push you to a place
           where you don't want to go.

SANDRA   You're afraid.

KEITH   Not Dougie.

SANDRA   It would be easier if I left, wouldn't it?

KEITH   That's crazy talk.

DOUG   I never said that.

SANDRA   Part of you wants me to leave and never come back.
           (*beat*) It would be less painful.

DOUG   Don't put words in my mouth.

SANDRA   (*beat*) We don't have to speak in order to be heard.

> SANDRA *locks eyes with* DOUG.

I'm not going anywhere.

KEITH   Good.

SANDRA   I have nowhere to go. No one would understand me. (*beat*) Understand us. The one thing she did.... One of the things she did was bring us closer together. There's no denying that. Had Tina been a regular kid you can bet we would have had a regular marriage. How many regular marriages head straight for the dustbin? They don't all end in divorce but they're covered with dust an inch thick. (*beat*) Not you and me. We were different. She made us different. She made us need each other in ways most husbands and wives couldn't begin to understand. (*pause*) Living with Tina was like learning a new language. (*pause*) I can't leave. (*beat*) I'll have no one to speak to.

KEITH   You don't mind the crazy talk. (*grins*) You, Ma'am, are courageous.

SANDRA   (*pause*) It's not all crazy talk, Keith.

KEITH   What do you mean?

SANDRA   (*to* DOUG) Tell him.

> KEITH *looks at* DOUG *expectantly.*

DOUG   Not here. Not now.

SANDRA   Why not? If you won't testify in court then say your piece here. You owe it to Keith.

KEITH What do you owe me?

>   *DOUG doesn't reply.*

SANDRA You built your ark. You did your gathering. Now you explain your choices.

KEITH I couldn't do it. I couldn't choose.

SANDRA Who goes. Who gets left behind. He deserves to know how you made that choice. (*beat*) Tell him.

>   *SANDRA exits through the shed door. The silence is palpable. DOUG turns and faces KEITH.*

DOUG (*pause*) There's something I want you to understand. (*pause*) Hoses.... Hoses aren't just for watering.

KEITH (*pause*) You used a hose. (*beat*) You used a hose.

DOUG I helped Tina.

KEITH Tina's dead.

DOUG She's not in pain. Not anymore. She went to sleep and never woke up. She died peacefully.

KEITH How do you know? How do you know how she was feeling? (*beat*) How do you know?

DOUG I held her in my arms.

KEITH Did you ask her if she wanted to die?

DOUG She couldn't speak. You know that.

KEITH You don't know that. You don't speak Tina.

DOUG Tina couldn't talk. Not the way you and I do.

KEITH   She could laugh. The puppets made her laugh.

DOUG   When?! When was the last time she laughed? Nothing we did could make her laugh. Not at the end. There was nothing to laugh at. They were going to operate again. Slice off a part of Tina's thighbone like they were carving up a turkey.

KEITH   Doctors make you better.

DOUG   Not always. There were going to be more operations, Keith. But the pain wouldn't have stopped. Nothing Dr. Kovacs did would stop the pain. Not completely. That's no way to live.

KEITH   How do you know what she wanted? You're not God.

DOUG   I'm her father.

KEITH   Some father.

DOUG   I would never hurt her.

KEITH   Killing hurts.

DOUG   She died in her sleep.

KEITH   You killed her like she was a dog. (*beat*) She couldn't protect herself. She couldn't fight back.

> *KEITH grabs the long-handled shears.*

DOUG   Put those down, Keith.

KEITH   You wanted to see what it was like. That's why you asked me to tie you up. To see what Tina's pain was like.

> *KEITH takes a stab at DOUG, but he dodges the shears.*

DOUG   Put them down.

KEITH   (*beat*) Was it like this?

> KEITH *stabs DOUG with the shears, managing to cut into flesh.*

DOUG   You fucking crazy?

> DOUG *covers the nasty cut with a handkerchief.*

KEITH   A freak, right?

DOUG   That's…. That's not what I meant.

KEITH   That's what people say. A freak of nature. Like Tina.

DOUG   You're not Tina.

KEITH   You killed her because she was different.

DOUG   She was in pain.

KEITH   You're in pain. Should I kill you?

DOUG   Don't be ridiculous.

KEITH   Why shouldn't I kill you?

DOUG   Not all pain is the same. (*beat*) This will heal. Tina was never going to heal. Ever. Do you understand that?

KEITH   That's why you killed her? Because she wouldn't heal? I'm never going to heal. Not completely. (*beat*) Are you going to kill me, too?

DOUG   Don't be ridiculous.

KEITH   Stop saying that!

> *KEITH lunges toward DOUG. DOUG avoids being cut again.*

DOUG   All right. Okay. You're... you're not being ridiculous. (*beat*) I'm not going to kill you.

KEITH   How do I know?

DOUG   Keith...

KEITH   How do I know?!

DOUG   I'd never do that.

KEITH   You killed Tina. I have pain. Kill me.

> *KEITH points the shears toward himself.*

Kill me.

DOUG   No.

KEITH   Kill me like you killed her.

DOUG   I'm not going to kill you!

KEITH   Kill me. Kill my pain!

> *KEITH attempts to cut himself with the shears. DOUG intervenes.*

Kill me, kill me, kill me!

DOUG   No! No, no, no, no, no, no, no!

> *They scuffle and struggle. The fighting intensifies until they both collapse.*

KEITH   Don't kill me. Please don't kill me.

> *DOUG holds KEITH.*

I don't want to die.

DOUG   I don't want you to die.

KEITH   I'm scared.

DOUG   I'm holding you.

KEITH   Don't hurt me.

DOUG   Never.

KEITH   You hurt her. You hurt me.

DOUG   I see that now.

KEITH   I don't understand. I don't understand. (*pause*) Tina. Tinatinatinatinatinatinatinatina…

> *DOUG releases KEITH, who runs out of the shed. The lights fade as DOUG tends to his wounds.*

> *Lights up on DOUG as he unscrews a small section of the ark. SANDRA enters and simply watches.*

DOUG   It'll never fit into my cell.

SANDRA   That's not funny.

DOUG   It's the truth. I'm taking a small piece with me instead.

SANDRA   Why?

DOUG   To remind me.

SANDRA   Of her?

DOUG   (*pause*) To remind me my intentions were good.

SANDRA   No one's ever questioned your intentions, Doug.

DOUG   You have.

SANDRA   Not your intentions. Your choice.

DOUG   When someone you love is being tortured, you have to intervene.

SANDRA   You think it's that simple?

DOUG   Don't judge my love. I had enough of that in the courtroom. "You didn't love her enough." That was the real verdict. "If you really loved your daughter, you never would have…". (*pause*) They will never understand.

SANDRA   I don't. Not completely. (*beat*) Neither do you.

DOUG   I know where I stand.

SANDRA   You don't, or you'd never need a reminder of your good intentions.

> *DOUG stops taking the ark apart.*

Leave the ark here, in one piece. (*beat*) Take the dove.

DOUG   That's Keith's call. (*pause*) I'll miss him. (*beat*) And you.

SANDRA   And if you had to do it again?

DOUG   (*pause*) I'd do it. Only this time I'd stay in the truck.

> *DOUG walks over to SANDRA and kisses her.*
> *KEITH enters and stands at the doorway.*

You worried about the cut? (*beat*) I only needed a few stitches.

> *KEITH doesn't reply. He grabs a pair of small shears and uses the stepladder to stand beneath the mourning dove. He clips one string at a time until the dove is hanging by its neck. He hesitates, then cuts the last string. The dove falls into his free hand. KEITH drops the shears, walks toward the shed door and waves goodbye to SANDRA. He turns, locks eyes with DOUG, and exits*

SANDRA   Ten years is a long time.

DOUG   We don't know if it's going to be ten years.

SANDRA   Jail is for criminals. You're not a criminal.

DOUG   No.

> *TINA's breathing slowly surfaces, at once both present and haunting.*

SANDRA   (*pause*) Sitting in court, day after day, I kept thinking of Tina when she was first born. (*pause*) This one night, I don't think she was more than three weeks old. She'd been crying up a storm so you took her in your arms and danced with her. You danced and you hummed and… she fell asleep. Then you brought her to me. You looked at me and you… (*pause*) I've never repeated it. I couldn't bring myself to say it. But you might as well have tattooed it on my forehead. (*beat*) You kissed Tina. You kissed me. Then you said, "We're going to outlive her, so we have to out-love her." (*beat*) We did, didn't we?

> *Tina's breathing envelops DOUG and SANDRA.*

DOUG   There was no end to our love.

TINA's breathing stops.

SANDRA   She loves you still.

DOUG   (*pause*) You think?

Lights fade to black.

Afterword

Mourning Dove began as a commissioned radio play for CBC's "Morningside", directed with great care by Gregory J. Sinclair and first broadcast in 1996. Inspired by a true story of a father who killed his severely disabled daughter in the name of love, Gregory and I never set out to recreate the facts of a story that made national headlines and continues, to this day, to spark passionate debates. Rather, the seeds of an actual event were transplanted into a fictitious world where motivations could more fully be explored, characters could be created to challenge hard-won beliefs, and family dynamics could be laid bare. Selected as the Canadian entry in the inaugural WorldPlay Festival showcasing English-language radio drama, *Mourning Dove* has been broadcast in the U.S., Britain, Australia, New Zealand, Hong Kong and South Africa and translated into Slovak.

When Dave Carley, a colleague and accomplished playwright for both stage and radio, suggested I adapt *Mourning Dove* for the stage, I resisted. Much of a radio drama's power is generated by a listener's imagination, as colours and textures are added to a landscape drawn by the playwright. This is particularly true in a play like *Mourning Dove*, where the role of the disabled daughter was distilled into her laboured breathing. To hear Tina breathe is to know her character. To see her on stage would reduce her spirit to a shopping list of misguided concerns: What would she look like? How would her twisted limbs be positioned to suggest pain? I felt these kinds of questions would derail the story's dramatic thrust and turn a character into a sideshow. Only when I realized I could borrow from the best of what radio has to offer did I pursue *Mourning Dove* as a stage play. I grew to believe that an essential character could be made real by marrying two elements—breath and light.

No sooner had I cleared one hurdle did I face several others. Adapting a radio play for the stage presents challenges that underscore the strengths and limitations of each genre. It took several drafts for the stage version of *Mourning Dove* to find its footing, a trial-and-error process made less arduous with a guiding hand from Richard Rose, then artistic director of Necessary Angel Theatre Company in Toronto. After listening to the radio play Richard agreed to offer dramaturgical input in the play's journey toward a stage production. Input can be invaluable, but what about income? Bills can't be paid with rewrites, and I am indebted to Necessary Angel and three arts agencies for the funding they provided while I wrote—and rewrote—*Mourning Dove*: the Canada Council for the Arts, the Ontario Arts Council and the Toronto Arts Council.

The drafts written while I was a playwright-in-residence at Necessary Angel led to a two-week workshop directed by Richard Rose that featured the insights of R.H. Thomson, Maggie Huculak, Fabrizio Fillipo, Victor Ertmanis and Caroline Gillis. The workshop led to a staged reading, with Kathryn Westoll as stage manager, in January 2002. The play had come a fair distance by then but was still too wedded to the radio play, or anchored to small details I had gleaned from the story that served as its inspiration. A comment by R.H. Thomson proved to be a turning point in the play's genesis. He linked the dove—introduced in the radio play and preserved in the adaptation—to the story of Noah's Ark. At first, I resisted the suggestion that the Noah story be woven into the play; it felt like a playwright using a heavy hand to nail a metaphor onto a script. But it made perfect sense for Doug Ramsay, a character who internalised his emotions, to harness the Noah story as a way of conveying his unspoken intentions. Two characters from the radio play and earlier stage drafts that I had once thought vital to the story—a medical doctor and police officer—were dropped. Puppets fashioned by Doug and Keith to entertain and engage Tina were introduced.

A timely opportunity to present the radically reworked script arose at a week-long workshop held at the University of Lethbridge in April 2002. Professor Brian Parkinson oversaw the Canadian Plays in Development program and chose *Mourning Dove* as a work worth examining. I spent an invaluable week with Richard Rose and a class of enthusiastic students shaping the script and getting it up on its feet at a staged reading. The Lethbridge workshop gave birth to more changes that were showcased later that year at the National Showcase of New Plays in Philadelphia, sponsored by the National New Play Network and hosted by InterAct Theatre.

Brian Parkinson, the personification of grace, chose to produce an earlier version of *Mourning Dove* in Lethbridge in March 2003. He knew I felt the play was incomplete but believed its strengths outweighed its shortcomings and included it in his season at New West Theatre. This was a gift: to see a work staged, knowing the clay of the script is still wet and can be reshaped. Watching the cast—Jeff Carlson, Erica Hunt, Ben Meuser and Misty Kozac— bring the script to life in a full-scale production was like meeting long-lost relatives whose stories are in your bones.

Scripts evolve. Characters grow. Artistic directors move on. Richard Rose left Necessary Angel, the dynamic company he had founded, when he was appointed artistic director at Tarragon Theatre. As is often the case, a script nurtured at one theatre dies on the vine at another. Disappointment, long an occupational hazard of the trade, was short-lived. In December 2003 I decided to stage my own reading of the play, in the hopes of generating interest in the wider theatre community. I rented a theatre in a library and, with R.H. Thomson on board to direct the reading, attracted a stellar cast. Fab Fillipo agreed to revive the role of Keith he had brought to life at an earlier workshop, and I was given three more reasons to believe in the boundless talent of Canadian actors: Ron White, Stavroula Logothettis, and Mary Francis Moore.

The reading caught the attention of Lorne Pardy, artistic director at the Great Canadian Theatre Company in Ottawa. He asked to read the latest version of the play—fifteen drafts and counting— which had changed significantly from the workshop he had seen some two years earlier. A few months later, Lorne had committed to direct the premiere of *Mourning Dove*. He assembled an inspiring cast to play Doug and Sandra: Tim Webber and Kate Hurman both brought great skill, compassion and commitment to the roles. Ben Meuser—who had played Keith in both the staged reading and production in Lethbridge—was offered the opportunity to bring his passion and gifts for the role and made his professional debut in *Mourning Dove*. And what of Tina? I had long believed that Tina had to be real, and not a recording. I knew the cast would respond in very different ways if an actor was there—in rehearsals and off-stage during the run—than if Tina was simply a disembodied voice piped in through speakers.

After a bit of to-ing and fro-ing—artistic directors always have one eye on a balance sheet—Lorne agreed. Stephanie Burchell, a student at the Ottawa School of Speech and Drama, became Tina: never 'seen' but always there.

In addition to a marvellous cast, the creative team at GCTC worked their magic and transformed a script into an experience. Leigh Ann Vardy's lighting, Duncan Morgan's score, Kim Neilsen's design, Sarah Feely's wardrobe and props: each played their part in contributing to a very satisfying whole. Shainna Laviolette was a reminder that a stage manager, the unsung heroes of the theatre world, is the mortar that keeps a production from falling apart. Lorne Pardy took on the challenge of presenting a play by an unknown playwright, presenting a work that is not, at first blush, an easy sell. It is hard to imagine throngs rushing to see a play that is, ostensibly, about a father who kills his disabled daughter. Lorne knew it was much more than that, I am grateful that he embraced the story as artfully as he did.

All plays are, essentially, a work in progress. Each time a play is remounted it is in reinterpreted. Each time it is read, it is re-imagined. But a play also has a core that is immutable. Each draft of *Mourning Dove* brought me closer to ageless questions about complex moral choices, a place where tidy resolutions can never take root. The journey has been long but gratifying. The journey was made all the richer because it was shared. And the journey is not yet over, as long as there are those willing to ask questions that beget more questions.

Emil Sher
Toronto, May 2005

Emil Sher works include stage plays, screenplays, radio dramas and essays. Previous plays include *Sanctuary*, a one-act play that has been staged in Canada, the U.S., Britain and Australia and *Derailed* (created with Stiletto Company). *Café Olé*, his first feature film, was honoured by the Writers Guild of Canada as one of the top ten scripts of 2002. Emil's radio plays have been broadcast around the world, and three have been collected in *Making Waves*. He has been a playwright-in-residence at Necessary Angel Theatre Company and the Lorraine Kimsa Theatre for Young People. Current projects include an adaptation of *Hana's Suitcase* and several radio dramas for the CBC. *Beneath the Banyan Tree* (Theatre Direct Canada) and *Bluenose*, plays for young audiences, will tour in upcoming seasons. To learn more about Emil's work, please visit his website at emilsher.com.